Light in All Directions

Light in All Directions

poems by

Brandon Cesmat

Poetic Matrix Press

Front Cover Image Credit: NASA, ESA, and H. Weaver (Johns Hopkins University/Applied Physics Lab)
Comet 17P/Holmes Hubble Image - October 31, 2007

Back Cover photo by Dorothy Steinbeck

Copyright © 2009 by Brandon Cesmat

ISBN: 978-0-9824276-4-4

All rights reserved. No part of this book may be used or reproduced in any manner whatsoever without written permission, except in the case of quotes for personal use and brief quotations embodied in critical articles or reviews.

Poetic Matrix Press
www.poeticmatrix.com

Acknowledgments

Versions of these poems have appeared in the following publications:

Canary: "Pine Speak"; *Hiss Quarterly:* "Loading the Dishwasher"; *Inverted Pyramid:* "Between Thorns"; *Magee Park:* "Commie Backtalk," "Crime Medicine," "For Every Too Little, a Too Much," "Survival Shadows" and "Voices Sift"; *Mise-en-Poem:* "My Brother's Nightmare"; *Moon Won't Leave Me Alone:* "Morning After All-Saint's Eve"; *mo+th:* "Cough of Dissipation"; *Nest of Freedom:* "The Next Dream"; *Other Voices International Project:* "Coca-Cola Is Guilt," "Fire Mind" and "Turn"; *Pemmican:* "Reagan Memorial Poem"; *Perigee:* "Lost Dog"; *Poetic Oceans:* "Pine Speak"; *Poetry Conspiracy:* "Night Classes"; *Poetry Super Highway:* "Cold Heart," "February Rain," "On the Broken Coast" and "Where Have All the Bulls Gone?"; *Prism:* "Discussing Labor at the Feast," "Difficult Colors" and "Aphasic Confession"; *Red River Review:* "Light in All Directions"; *ROADSpoetry:* "Dream Damage" and "Shell of Heaven"; *San Diego Poetry Annual:* "The Answer," "Goat Laughter," "Revolution of Flame" and "Turn"; *San Gabriel Valley Poetry Review:* "Flow Between Storms" and "Invasive Hunger"; *Walker Creek: Collected Poems:* "Long Distance"; *Word Traffic:* "Man on the Overpass," "Saturday A.M. Parade" and "Tongues of Dust"; *A Year in Ink:* "Men in Trees."

"Men in Trees" and "Witness Trees" were written for David Avalos' installation *Mi Corazón Escondido* at The Museum of the California Center for the Arts, Escondido.

Poetry text
GoudyOLSt BT
Frederic W. Goudy (1865–1947) was a prolific American type designer whose fonts include Copperplate Gothic, Kennerley, and Goudy Old Style.
In 1911, Goudy produced his first "hit," Kennerly Old Style, for an H. G. Wells anthology published by Mitchell Kennerly. His most widely used type, Goudy Old Style, was released by the American Type Founders Company in 1915, becoming an instant classic.

Poem subtitle is the title in music notation
Petrucci
Ottaviano Petrucci (June 18, 1466 – May 7, 1539) was an Italian printer. Petrucci is credited with producing, in 1501, the first book of sheet music printed from movable type: *Harmonice Musices Odhecaton*, a collection of chansons. He also published numerous works by the most highly regarded composers of the Renaissance, including Josquin des Prez and Antoine Brumel.

Poem titles
Lucida San
Lucida San is an extended family of related typefaces designed by Charles Bigelow and Kris Holmes in 1985.

Taken from Wikipedia® the free encyclopedia.

Contents

Fuse
Fire Mind 3
Vermont Street 5
The Dances 6
Counter Sunrise 8
Saturday A.M. Parade 10
February Rain 12
Unfinished Fountain 13
Discussing Labor at the Feast 14
Commie Backtalk 15
Long Distance 16
Fern Fractal 17
Pine Speak 18
Poisons 19
Cacodamemon 21
Morning After All-Saints' Eve 22
Loading the Dishwasher 23
Sloth 24
Voices Sift 25
Neuter 26
Lost Dog 27
A Cold Heart 28
Aphasic Confessions 29
Turn 32
Enrapture 33

Implode
Cough of Dissipation 37
Where Have All The Bulls Gone? 39
Survival Shadows 40
Tongues of Dust 41
On the Broken Coast 43
Night Classes 44
Revolution of Flame 47
In the coffee shop, leaves, ... 48

Men and Women I've Kissed 49
For Every Too Little, a Too Much 51
Goat Laughter 53
Coca-Cola Is Guilt 54
Silver Surfaces 55
Last Love 56
The Next Dream 57
Tuolumne Lines 58
My Brother's Nightmare 59
Difficult Colors 61
Hymn of Enough 63
Invasive Hunger 66
Man on the overpass, ... 67
Creases 68
Young man pedaling 69
Bon Voyage 70
Shell of Heaven 71
Flow Between Storms 72
Another Way To Say "God's Eyes" 73
Hojas y Ojos: Leaves and Eyes 74
Witness Trees, 2007 75
Men in Trees 76
Hotel Carrera, 1974 78
After Dusk 79
Crime Medicine 81
Dream Damage 82
The Reagan Memorial Poem 83

Radiate

In the Memory Market 89
Darlin', when our figure-eight starts 91
The Answer 92
Light in All Directions 93

Author Bio

Dedication

For my mother Donna Sheryl Cesmat
who carried snakes off the road and gentled horses.

Fuse

Fire Mind

October firestorm rolls west over
the rim of Eden Creek Canyon.
Smoke from hundreds of homes, barns,
photos and lives of twenty-one neighbors
roils in incense of white sage
sacred to tribal people on two reservations
now ablaze, their outlawed spring burns
resurrected brutally in autumn.
Recognizing the ghost of smoke releases me
to accept losing everything so that when
our house emerges after fire, only planks of
patio on fire, I resist calling it "blessing."

That night, hot spots burn around canyon,
the only lights there until neighbors rebuild—
power lines ignited like fuses,
exploding suburbs in the brush—
and above spot fires, stars
calling back thousands of others, dark insisting.

The day after fire, I walk the rim,
first time in twenty years. Consoling neighbors
I'd never met as they sift ashes over concrete foundations,
I trespass freely to the east,
catch five goats, two pigs, a cat with
burnt paws. I shoot two horses without hooves,
their lungs singed, the blood they breathed
the only moisture within miles. I shoot
into another mind that becomes mine.
The fire: the rifle, and my hand: the bullet.
I follow a trajectory heartless as flames over so many.

Next week at a funeral, people flow through my arms.
I survive to hold them, open my cage of ribs.
Their sobs become my heartbeat, their tears: my blood.
My warmth from pressure of motion,
the same heat Santa Anas raise crossing the Mojave.
The town weeps itself dry while I wonder,
where are my tears of survival?

Each March, I burn brush. The flame at
the matchtip, the shape of an orange tear.
Neighbors watch. Every spring a warning.

Vermont Street

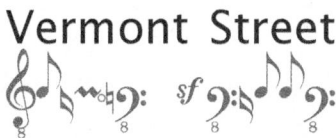

Our home on Vermont Street—
named after a state I've never visited—
my memory of that house belongs to my mother.

Once every two or three years, she asks if I remember
the intruder or the police, have I recovered the memory
of the darkened hallway with a gas heater at one end?
Then the flames go out. On the wooden floor the weight of
someone's foot, and when the heater lights again,
the silhouette of a man.

From her place on the bed, she almost calls out,
"What are you doing home" because the shadow is
the height and build of her husband in Vegas on business.

She pretends to sleep and prays until it walks toward my room.
I don't remember the intruder or the policeman
whose gun I asked to see. I don't remember that night.
She reminds me the doors were locked from the inside,
reminds me so often that I believe I remember the keyhole.
Only a poltergeist could seep in, she knows.

Between the backyard fence and hedge one July afternoon,
lying in their shade and watching the back door on Vermont Street,
I hid from my parents. Who else would look for me?
They want to bring me indoors
where they believe I will be safe.
I remember the fence on Vermont Street
and learning to climb it, what some
neighbors call, "trespass."

The Dances

I.
The girls in jr. high who taught us how to slow dance,
the work of patience. Oh, to kiss each one of them again,
softly, not trying to get French on them right away.

II.
In Valle Guadalupe, Fidel & Maria insisted I dance, so
I chose Enariena for her long black hair and eyes.
As we stepped together for a couple of songs,
we talked about carnival prizes and both sides of the border
while the old women sat on the wall around the plaza,
sipping vino mescal with sugar and hot water, watching.

III & IV.
At the manifestación in Managua, circles formed
in the middle of thousands for a man and woman
to meet in the middle. The men pushed me
toward a compra whose name I never learned.
In the noise, we couldn't hear, so
we danced and smiled glad, estadounidense to Sandinista.
Years later in an officers' club for my cousin's wedding,
a sullen ripple opens the moment
I recognize the unnecessary graves beneath our steps.

V.
Leroy nods me into the plaza. With my rattle,
and feet, I keep the beat.
The women facing me say I've got it,
and I feel they're right, we feel it through
our feet. Ah, for all the dancers.

VI.
Then the photo of my ex-wife and I dancing at my brother's wedding while she was already with her new partner. The camera caught her looking at me with love. I would cut it in half if I didn't need some evidence that every dance, if we keep dancing, is peace two or more at a time.

Counter Sunrise

On our first date, when I came out of the waves,
she'd taken my clothes, so I wrapped ice plant around me.
The bluffs beneath the homes would erode in eleven years.
I dressed for her in whatever was nearby,
                                        disappeared into landscapes.

Between orange trees, spiked milkweed left
the skinny paths we walked through the grove.

One morning before school Grammy pointed to
where my belt buckle left holes in my shirt and said,
"That happens when you dress sloppy."

On a Mother's Day hike, our youngest son disappeared
into the boulders and emerged on a limb bridging
twenty feet over the creek. He didn't know enough to fear,
so while she hid her eyes, I stood beneath him and
encouraged forward motion, the safest direction.

Smudges on our TV screen rebelled against digital clarity,
drew me close to examine a veil of—was it peanut butter
                                        or quesadilla?—
lacey grease, my children's fingerprints, unidentifiable to passersby.

I walked between the trees so the ranch foreman wouldn't see
my footprints in that grove where a boy about my age, my mother said,
once trespassed, and no one ever saw him again.
One afternoon when I was five, a gopher chased me. My father ran out,
stomped its head and threw it into the grove, disgusted at my screaming.
Grammy couldn't stand bare feet, yet she loved me. Do shoes make the man?
Or the woman? In her favorite canvas sneakers, she cut holes for corns.

Today, as I walked through the Beverly Center,
the maintenance man made me remember El Salvador's disappeared,
so I bought nothing,
no coffee, no lemonade, no new shirt.
                                        I unbuckled nothing.

A week before our wedding we weaved between milkweed thistles
and felt Spanish Goat Heads sticking to the bottom of our shoes.
We stood on thorns and didn't disappear into the grove.
But there is a boy about my age who never came back.
Optimists say he moved with earth's spinning, counter to sunrise.
Forensic analysts could read his fingerprints on the leaves,
but without a missing person report filed or a body found,
                                                        no one bothers.
By now friction of the wind would have worn the clothes off his body
or he would have grown thin enough
                                          to walk through unscratched.

Saturday A.M. Parade

♪ (♯)𝄢: ♪□(♯)△ (♭)·♪♪. *mp*(♯)♪(♯)□♪

Two bicyclists on a back road
riding side by side, a tangent of conversation
between them—an invisible I-beam from
her mouth to his ear—balances their pedaling.

Bike guy's attention wobbles
over her bumpy words.
The hum of his tires murmurs in
constant agreement on octave below her voice.
He'd follow her muscles' flow if she led.

   Old man in the pick-up behind them slows to see
   if cycle-girl will pull ahead and leave a lane to pass.
   After a slow quarter-mile, he hopes one of her words
   will drift back to him so he can at least eavesdrop.
   The air rushing over her ears and the grumble in his motor
   have made them deaf to one another.
   Only the old man is lonely.

      Behind the truck, an intern late to work
      brakes on the cushion of space.
      This younger man's mind is not belted in and flies
      down the road so fast he doesn't even see the bicyclists,
      the beam between them or hear
      their bumpy words above the rumbling whoosh
      until the old man swings left and accelerates safely ahead

         so another young woman shuffling through
         cigarette smoke and Friday night's hangover
         makes her way onto the porch
         at the moment the four profiles stack-up: out front,
         a faded face of a bill, scowling over a steering wheel,
         the young woman, shiny in sweat, a coin heads-up like

the young man pedaling in profile and
steely intern chasing the parade.
Their momentum blows past the porch, so
the smoky woman stumbles one step in their direction.

February Rain

The worn gray wood of the deck
deepens into black beneath this rain.
The planks release their scent
as if, in drawing up the earth's moisture,
they remember being together before the saw.

On my drive to work, the rain falls faster, as if
it waited for me to come outdoors.
When I cut the engine,
the drops drumroll the roof
and blur the windshield,
a reminder to close my eyes and listen.
Outdoors, hissing or splashing tires
shush the tapping and touching
of everything.
Nevertheless, I distinguish
fallen leaves from green by their resonance,
loneliness from empathy, respectively.
Music came from days like these.

Outside, I close my eyes,
tilt my face up so
cold beats play my left cheek,
their voices changing as
I silently open and close my mouth.

Unfinished Fountain

My mother never collected stones smoothed by snowmelt.
She had my brothers and me load the trunk of her car with desert
stones broken into a jagged puzzle by the world's weight and heat,
their iron veins rusted red; she planned a fountain for them.
Five Aprils, tall weeds hid them in a pile; then
we moved them from home to home with us,
maxing out the car's shocks again and again, me
muttering until my brothers told me to shut up.

Since the firestorm I often look across the canyon where
a house burned down around river rocks stacked into a fireplace.
At night it stands out like a ghost of someone who lived there.
Why haul river stones into this dry chaparral for smoke to roll up?

I clacked the desert rocks together because
I desired to become a river that wore them smooth
before I left home, or as
our mother pushed around us
on her way to sea.
Instead, I rose into a chimney of desert shards for
a river of smoke to ripple through until lost in the sky.

Discussing Labor at the Feast

Agave roasted orange not from July
    but dug from a desert circle, swollen by monsoons,
        holding its breath of water against the hard pan,
disentangled and reburied with suns from cores of trees,
    while cooks boil nettles and sip tea off spoons.
        Smoke from roast venison baits the tribal chairman.

For dessert he asks, "Will professors strike?
    Are they wise enough to balance a balloon
        against the dropping price of carcinogens?"
Agave exhales steam, holds orange sugars worth a warm hike
    and an unpacking of Anza-Borrego's sand. Between back molars
        the professor clamps onto a grain of grit. To swallow or spit?

Commie Backtalk

Being the commie you call me,
I'm taking it all back:
diamond panes of glass for anyone who came to our front door.
I'm taking back Grampy's rub-downs after football practice.
You don't believe me? Sit down, let me massage your shoulders.

The glances at Sara Montoya's house
whenever I rode past. I'm taking them back.
The shine from her brown hair I'd forgotten until just now,
the boulder that Paradise Creek flows under.
I'm taking them back.
Don't try to stop me.

Every trail Gary Bates and I ever left through the brush,
we're rolling them up through the middle of homes,
property rights be damned.

The pisses over the canyon ledge every night,
I'm taking back those nocturnal pleasures
to add all together and hit the new casino on the other side.

Being the commie you call me,
I'm giving you everything I love:
the brown mare who carried me safely through childhood, like a mother,
the wedges of lasagna Grammy stacked just the way I liked them.
Everything I've taken, I redistribute.

Here, have a couple of notes I took off Jaco backstage at The Roxy
or a couple of rests I stole from Count Basie one night in Montreux.
They lifted them from America,
and God knows where she got them.

Long Distance

Grandad Damon, who parked beneath oaks down the road
and never knocked on our door,
who is creosote and clouds over the Mojave,
who is the warning light flashing on the tower,
whose wrinkles the roots of middle-class opportunity cut,
who was too humiliated to pull in our driveway,
who, once every six months, telephoned
long distance, drunk,
who told me beer is the secret to his chili recipe,
who amazed his son by shooting doves for supper
as their car flushed them into the prairie sky,
who turned back on a hunt because
my father couldn't cross a fence line with a shotgun,
who turned back and kept going like a movie cowboy,
who left the body of a black man beneath a Texas bridge,
who set that man's ghost inside every empty whiskey,
and found that ghost in his pocket every morning,
no matter where the spirit went,
who became that black ghost
who now calls me over telephone lines he suspended West,
calls from the grave to say, "How you look like me."

Fern Fractal

In February I punch my clenched fist
against the field crusted with snow.
However tightly I close on myself,
I cannot force my way into the blue.
I wait for the snow to collapse around me,
rush beneath me, and I stand
against the sky and in defiance of dirt.
In peace I spread horizontally,
submit the fronds to the blue, yet on my palm
the leaves curl tight. "Open," I whisper.

Pine Speak

mp♭♮♪ *sf p*♪(♯).

I stand here by the grace of my scars.
See the burl on my trunk's downhill-side where
I isolated an infection into
                        the pupil of a wooden eye.
All I have to say is, "See?"
So, see the vertical line of my trunk
                        broken by boughs.

I am implicated by gravity's law:
the dead bird beneath my limbs and
the needles I've dropped over him;
I'd do as much for you.
How well do I remember that bird?
Not well, they all move so fast.
My male and female pinecones
                        on the ground together,
sex, sex, sex everywhere.
Where is the love in this law?

Still, I claim innocence.
                Indifference is one of my gifts.
I am in the business of enfolding light,
absorbing water and minerals,
releasing my all as seeds.

I'm not proud of my scars.
My wood can rot or burn for all I care.
I tell you we are both blessed
to have made it this far
with anything to lose.

Poisons

mp♭ s♭s

Poison oak enforces property rights
in that SoCal town with a custom home for every hilltop,
water supply be damned.

Though the legal way to my house was a busy road
with a thousand cul-de-sacs, a fancy way to say "dead-end."
Even though there was no trail through the sumac grove,
I wanted that shortest distance of a straight line
between my hike's turning point and home.

Two days later, I remembered that arroyo—so quiet and green,
the leaves not yet red—when sores erupted first on my left ankle.

The welts on my right thigh must've come from crossing my legs
while sitting around in my underwear,
the pustules on my right elbow from leaning on my knee.

While scratching the left ankle with a ball-point pen,
I saw the connected red dots spelled *"FOR SALE."*

I worked dot-to-dot on my left forearm,
which read, *"PROPERTY RIGHTS,"* while
the right wrist uncomfortably spelled, *"SPRAWL."*
Instead, I closed my legs; the rash on my thighs instructed to
"SUBSIDIZE LIABILITY," so I wondered how.
The next morning, pustules beneath my waistband
answered, *"PRIVATIZE PROFIT."*

Later in that valley, people burned to death on
the legal road beside the fire station.
"These things have a way of working themselves out,"
the pastor says, and I take that as a blessing to scratch.

The burned grove forgave my insistent footsteps on
a trail less poison than the broken shoulders of road
so congested there isn't even room for smoke.

Cacodamemon

I do not "play" the Devil's advocate;
I represent him and any devil who retains me.
Lucifer's secrets remain so by attorney-client privilege.
For example, I cannot say what
special Mother's Day gift he might have purchased…
but there, I've already said too much.
Yes, Satan—like all evil—has a mother,
and she's been happily married all these centuries.

Of course I over-bill him hourly because
it pleasantly fulfills his low expectations.
I tell my clients how to confess their ignorance.
I am unaware of any lies. I admit freely
the distance between "not guilty" and "innocent" is
divinely beyond me.
In such a marvelous, mysterious world,
who will disbar me for what I don't know
here in the throes of such sweet amnesia?

The Devil is not an attorney,
he is my client.
And me?
I am, as are all lawyers, the hired help,
or to get to the bottom line, I am
as much advice as any Satan can afford.

Morning After All-Saints' Eve

How good it is to be alive after the horror of last night,
driving the children around the dark neighborhoods,
glad to see the few pumpkins, brainless but luminous.

I check the treats to make sure they're wrapped and
wonder if it wasn't an underemployed dentist who
slipped the first razor-blade into an apple.
Could people who open their doors be more dangerous
than those who hide on the live side of their TV?

We passed a pack of teens in no costumes, unless
they wanted to show us that horrific moment of transformation when
the mask of childhood slips and reveals the cruel grown-up creature
smoking, sulking, hulking, drunken, humping, thumping after dark.

Now in the morning paper, a victim-bites-vampire headline
about a Cuban spy expelled from The Pentagon.
Watching cartoons, my son still wearing plastic fangs
munches a Snickers that contains no embargoed sugar,
and my daughter, still wearing her diaphanous wings,
flits between us, practicing for the after life.

Loading the Dishwasher

My wife does the dishes
after I cook. This is our arrangement.
She sponges the stain of
watermelon juice I left on the counter.
I don't have to watch. I can go read
or change the water on the orange trees.
But I have a stack of plates from the table.
The bottom two wiped clean by biscuits,
the top three still greasy.
She slides them all into the water to soak
and pinches a hard grain of rice that never cooked,
throws it into the garbage pail that's become a bouquet
with what's left of green onions and cauliflower leaves.
She hates our arrangement, though it was her idea.
I squeeze in beside her at the sink.
We push each other to load the dishwasher.
She slaps me with the dishtowel, then
smiles as we leave the kitchen so clean
no one can tell that we've eaten.

Sloth

lies on the living room floor
with the curtains closed.
I stand over him and yell,
"No lunch until you get up,"
as if volume translates to pure energy.
Sloth rises and faces me.
In his gaze, I yawn, shake my head clear
and push him toward the front yard.
We shuffle as far as the welcome mat
before leaning forehead-to-forehead
as if listening to one another's dreams.
"See," Sloth whispered, "Isn't this enough?"

Voices Sift

Now that I have died
and the electricity of my mind has quieted,
I can see the spaces between atoms.
The solitude of my world has spread:
the skin over my hand,
the boulder in the shade
diaphanous.
It no longer hurts to stare at the sun.

I cannot see the living except as smears.
Their breath the color of August grass
swirls through mouths and nostrils,
seeps into outlines of musculature,
disintegrates in green sparkles.

By their heights and postures, I recognize my family.
They move together, embrace and blur.
I reach as if they were a blanket I could wrap around me,
but my fingers cannot find the edge.

My wife's mind ripples in the wind of her ideas.
I place my ear to her lips,
but her voice passes through me.
Outside our backdoor, I sift into the boulder
resonating with old sound waves.
I silence myself to hear my family speak,
but only my words roll past again
when I am at last ready to listen.

Neuter

My wife brought the dogs back from the vet,
well, most of the dogs. Forrest, a black lab,
and Toshiro, a coyote-looking stray,

came home neutered. I watched
for the changes that were not supposed to come.
They wagged their tails, and my wife said, "See?"

But I didn't. Nothing swung between their legs
when they trotted down the driveway;
they didn't roll onto their backs to sun their genitals.

Forrest—named for Forrest Gump—ran less and grew fat;
Toshiro—named for the seventh samurai—ceased to swagger.
They seemed less competitive, "And what's wrong with that,"

my wife asked. The dogs stayed home,
the arroyos and groves apparently no longer on their minds;
no more dogs running loose, another way to say, "Free."

"They will be happier," she said, and I imagined it.
What if the geldings are the happy ones. Nothing to give
but presence, no mating because life depends on it,

no desire to wander. All the castrated balls incinerated,
I hope. I hate to think of them stacked somewhere like
nuclear waste. No one searching for them, everyone home.

Lost Dog

When the boy's dog didn't come
home from hunting squirrels or rabbits,
he rode on a brown mare
in the hills above the ranch,
singing the name, "Ti-ger! Here boy!" as he looked.
His parents already knew
that the ranch foreman had dumped the body in
a baranca just below the crest.
So many shadows rose beneath the sycamores,
the boy never saw his dog lying in the leaves.
He called until the name became a lament.
Those two weeks in the hills belong to Tiger.
Finally, his mother told him not to call anymore,
but a ghost of that boy is still up there,
riding the ghost of that mare
every place that he left his voice.
No one can touch them.

A Cold Heart

The symmetry from my heart of dust
branches out as a snowflake.
This is the shape of my love
that I can't explain and you don't understand,
but the mirrored evidence shows
I am enigmatically whole for you.
In this dry cold I have pulled all nearby moisture to me
for one moment. Quick, see me, this one side of me
that rings in the quiet, then melts into the rushing hum.

Aphasic Confessions

(b)♩ᵖᵈ(♯)ˢᵇ C ♩ᶜ♮ᶠᵈ 'ˢˢᵇ ♩ˢ

I.
On the oncology ward, I pass
the bed of a man with many women
around it, reading from the Bible,
praying that he be healed.

The women lean into him
as if to warm themselves.
I look for some recognition
in the ash of his face;
his blank stare pulls them close;
they follow.

To my father's bed, I push my way through no one and
the nostalgia for the bitterness my mother and I feel.
I rub his hands, the friction of our skin warm for a moment,
not like the bile in my belly I carried
over a distance that will not close now forever.
His aphasic speech clutters a clear understanding of any confession.
I'm glad just to have caught up with him at this hospital bed,
stand beside it as if it were a boat, push
and let go, this time at peace to see him drift off.

II.
While her ex-husband's life disentangled,
                              she refused
to pick up one strand of the man's life
and weave it into place, not for their son who
visited her with news of how the brain tumors grew while
the chemo broke him down.
She had her own pains in the hip and knee and
spine, one affliction entwined with the other in
overcompensation so she could barely move around her house.

On bad days she cultivated her losses,
asked if Nancy—the other ex-wife only three-years older than her son—
or any of the other women had been to visit him.
No one. Not from work. None of their other children. No one
would be the angel to rock him across into Hell
or Heaven, wherever he went unforgiven.
Did he repent of all the women, the squandered family
business, all children alienated except this son
who visited her twice a week trying to revive her love
just so it could die again?
                                        She limped away and laughed
when their son described the CAT scan of tumors as knots in wood.
If only her ex had wood for brains instead of the skill to
engineer affairs across their hometown and to foreign cities.

She would not be the woman to caress the body her son described:
atrophied on the left side, bloated from Dilantin on the right,
his one good hand—the word *good* made her laugh again—
his one good hand tied to the rail
so it wouldn't pull out his feeding tube.

She sees her husband grow as he dies in her son's eyes.
Doesn't my son remember, she wonders,
my husband left me.
He's leaving again.
Does anyone remember as I do?
Look at my smile, she wants to say, see?
Can you imagine how beautiful I was?
                                                She shrinks as she lives.
She will not be one of those women leaning over a hospital bed
as if to sense some heat or to keep their man warm, or as if
they were dying with him.
She will not look for one ember to rekindle from inevitable ash.

There will be no healing. She feels the knot solid
behind her chest. She has encased it.
It does not hurt.
Her breath flows easily around it.

Turn

Dad, I didn't care that the waves brought no grunion.
I was happy anyway beside you in the dark,
brave enough not to hold your hand.
Remember we ran with the current, hoping to find
the fish slicing their eggs into the sand.
I would probably not remember the longhaired stranger
who handed me a fish
if after he ran to the next wave,
you had not turned toward the parking lot and said,
"Some hippy gave you your first fish.
I should've been the one. Dirty hippies."
For a moment, I hung back in the waves,
the fish heavy with the dark you'd covered it with,
the dark I recognized when you left my mother.
I've been devouring that stranger's fish all this time,
pulling back first from you whenever we hug.

Enrapture

As I grow in the field with other sunflowers,
we turn to mimic our namesake,
our heads growing heavy.
A thought splits into a thousand seeds that
spiral into the white hole of my heart.
I stagger to hold all, but
just before I wearily release them,
I remember being a seed,
that I broke the hold and swirled into the world
amazed at my momentum and the mystery of where it came from.

Implode

Cough of Dissipation

My sons didn't like to run with me because
they wanted to take breaks and I pushed.
Now, I'm sitting back with a cold one and
kickin' it, as they say (though no one says

what gets kicked). We are what we dissipate.
Backlit mountains measure the day once more,
graph the earth's revolution against the dark,
Thursday's counter-reformation against Wednesday.

If the gun-barrel is not the barrel but the trachea,
then every soldier who lives by the Lord, dies by
the Lord. Graves labor every holiday. Fate invoices
the young man frozen on the edge of the high-

jive. I'll give you what I've got, though lately,
I can't seem to give away my cough.
One tired evening, I'll convulse myself
inside out and inhale the world with

all its celestial mottling. Hold the coil of morning.
From a bird's-eye perspective, civilization's fabric is
a crushed place to validate, but I won't give in.
The house saturated with barbeque smoke is mine.

I've smudged it on holidays and must admit
I worry my sons' circulatory system will resemble my grill.
I feel this guilt years before their hearts give out.
I ate the potatoes Grampy fried for me because,

I'm telling you brother, he wanted them himself,
wanted them in the worst way. You've been there,

haven't you? When you want something for someone
because you know damn sure it ain't coming your way,

not even if you send an engraved invite every spring?
Our wedding invitations gave the wrong address so half
my friends never arrived; the ceremony would've swallowed me whole,
but half of me never got to the end of the gun. My wife

never got shot either. If she pertinently ran a red light into me,
imagine the hell we'd pay trying to collect insurance.
I'd slice that day into right angles and deny I knew the driver,
claim someone jacked my DNA and dissipated my identity.

Where Have All The Bulls Gone?

Most evenings, I'm glad to head home
after a long hot afternoon canoeing far from
my American city with its herd of bulls
      stampeding from limos,
           through lobbies
                and into board rooms,
looking for cows of cash.
Not even neckties can hold them back.

After those cows fatted for The Last BBQ,
the bulls roam from their homes on the range.
Everywhere they go, piles of evidence.
You can smell it in the Senate and
see it on newspapers.

I tried to get away
and relax on this creek,
but find myself floating alone
with the current pulling me home.
I'm reluctant to dip my palms in and paddle,
now that this creek looks so much like downtown
except there are no bulls nearby to blame.

Survival Shadows

sf ⌣♪♭V(♯)◢ *sf* ♩(♯)▢∞*s*

Could I regret the skin, after forty-one autumns of
compromise wove wrinkles into her map?

My sullen faith laments the cord of creation torn apart,
knotted spheres dropped as evidence of a cosmic crime.

I recognize nothing in the braided roots pulled so I might survive.
Faith dissipates in the shadow of regret.

I no longer remember the identity of muscles,
the ridges of the shell constant under tides.

Prayers, infiltrate this poem.
I would ask characters their identity before I would ask a friend his.

A stumble on a twelve-tone scale splinters the arc of no lyrics.
We burrow by design. No regrets, no shadows.

Tongues of Dust

At the wake, they won't stop saying my name.
That's the point, I guess, to keep me from drifting too far.
To make me stay, my mother tells
how fine I was to her,
sheds a story about how I drove her to lunch but
neglects to say I yelled at her in the car.

Echoes of my voice fill the living room.
My mother pauses as if she hears.
My sentences are the stems of roses
without blooms. My middle son has
nothing to say. His anger quakes. He blurs.
My fingers wrap around his time, so
I let go and push away like a cloud around a mountain;
it shimmers silver, black and red in this evening of grief.

Mourners' words pass me close
as if I'm hitchhiking a highway and
know the cargo of the truck trailers speeding by,
the only pulse left to me.

During a pause in conversation, I glide into my old room
and fall through the bed.
I'm heavily lost with the weight of dust until
someone says my name and inhales me;
I float on memory through them and
understand in Hell people don't touch.

Finally, my brother says,
"His opinions made him blind."
He's glad I'm quiet now,
so am I.

The haunting ends when they exhale on their ways home.

Outdoors, I drift where no strangers breathe my name.
Oh, the divine listening to unfamiliar voices,
to overhear what I don't understand.
At last quiet.
At last prepared to acquire the souls of enemies
and balance them like tides of one ocean.

On the Broken Coast

Just before this world turns to face
me into the dim morning light, I see
one starfish sitting still,
stuck to a low tide stone,
not like its namesakes above,
their jagged jets of green or white pulsing.
I bend close to this starfish spread in five directions,
frozen in indecision, and wait for it to move.
This one star stopped while the rest
went with the tide. A complex thought
coming together in the balanced gravities
of universes that throw light
as far as they can.
When earth turns us to mid-morning,
the stare of the sun breaks the five fingers
so this one complexity, the one I noticed
this morning, slips beneath the incoming tide.
I imagine it waving as it parades past the swells.

Night Classes

(♮)♭ ♩ 𝄢: ₵⊄(♯)ss♩ 's

He freeways home from work so she can freeway to nightschool.
He freeways spaghetti to the table.
He freeways to the living room to turn off the TV and
        freeway the children to the table and to mind manners.
He freeways them to bed, then
        fast-lanes a term paper for his night class tomorrow.

She liberates herself from night class, then
        liberates her lover for a dinner break in his trailer.
She liberates a man who does not cook for nor
        clean up after children.
She liberates a man who does not study.
She liberates a man who has the time to listen to her as
        long as they keyhole afterward.
She liberates a man who tells how
        he went into her husband's work
        to talk about the weather.
She liberates a sadist
        and the worry that sadists make sloppy step-fathers.

At night school, he freeways into an old girlfriend
        who asks if he still musics.
She dances him over coffee.
He freeways to bed with her.
He freeways past any destination on the blueprints.
He musics a note in his journal. His mind freehands new map.

She liberates her husband's journal and
        lasers beneath the words
                that liberate her from blindness.
That evening she liberates her husband from his.

They straight-back in front of the children.
They slither into counseling.
Their stomachs twirl for several weeks.
Their bed statues at night.
They settle with silences, their children won't, so
        she walks counseling while he still slithers.
She spits out sadism.
He swallows curses.
She refuses to dance.
They satellite their destinations and
        statue in restaurants once a week.

        He pushes wad after
        wad of digested suffering out his ass and
        negotiates with Jesus to
        haul the holy shit away.
        One night they crumble laughter.
        The next day the shit disappears,
        just like The Ascension.

Another day he freeways into the revelation of
        who's a weather-talking sadist,
            and the shit is resurrected all around them.

He floats complaints at her above the children's heads.
He choirs complaints at her in the bedroom with the door shut.
They statue in the same bed between different covers.
They marathon the mud they will make in their children's minds.

One afternoon when the children avenue to their grandparents,
        he earthquakes into the bathroom where
        she waterfalls alone and
        from the steam trapped against the ceiling,
        love raptures down.

They make use of his vasectomy.
They crumble into one pile of dirt.
They drift in front of their children.
The children catalog mysteries about them.
They distance questions that would make them lie.

They statue, they crumble,
They statue, they crumble.
They roadside for a strong wind.

Revolution of Flame

The first trouble was not when Santa Ana winds blew
across our brutal October lawns, dry stubble mowed low
amidst chamise and ceanothus.

The first trouble was not a spark from an unknown tailpipe
or cigarette.

The trouble was the arrogance that took the flame
indigenous people gave on damp May mornings
every year of creation until 1798
when the Spanish governor banned burns.

We have built cages in the brush
and they all burned in October 2003, but
in November, wild cucumber vines emerged
like green spiders from the black ground.
Who would believe their white petals would be set free
by brown smoke and orange roars?
Who would have expected the seldom seen vines
to be the first to embrace the burned earth?

In the coffee shop, leaves,

long and wide like ones
Enrique cut from the rainforest for
our hats during a storm.
With lightning at that elevation, his machete
seemed like a bad idea awaiting inspiration.

The trails crisscrossed streams until
I didn't know where we were.
Near the mountain top, the storm lifted
as if to move out of our way, so we could see
where Rió Savegre flowed into the Pacific.

Wet with rain and sweat,
breathing hard, we sat for a few minutes
and he elaborated on the machismo and feminismo,
what was for me collaboration all around us,
was for him an eternal order of so many buds to pollinate.

We descended to the plantation,
those fields of prosperity cleared from
the forests of evolution,
neither side able to forget the other,
like true lovers who divorce.

A river of her cuts to the sea of my heart
and is lost in other currents.

I raise my espresso like a machete in a storm
to cut toward a wild idea or clear a plantation of reason.
I write coffee-shop oblivious, my neighbors strangers to me,
as this potted plant is to the scent of coffee
made foreign by roasting, importing and grinding,
strange as rain on leaves is to a river in the sea.

Men and Women I've Kissed

Sometime during my second year at college, Eva comes to a party
    at our apartment while her boyfriend was studying.
    I fall behind the couch and she falls on top of me.
    When I leave school at the end of the semester,
    I fail several ways.

Grampy sat in his car at my freshman football practice
    while he was out of the hospital for two weeks.
        On the way to the locker room, I leaned in his window
    to kiss his cheek. The guys, sweaty and winded in pads,
    just carried their helmets around us.
    He passed during wrestling season.

In kindergarten, I had a crush on Julie Snyder,
    who lived down a ranch road on the way to our house.
    She and her mother wore white go-go boots
    like Goldie Hawn's on the forbidden "Laugh-In,"
    which I watched while hidden behind the couch.
    Mom said Julie's parents were hippies and
    wasn't surprised when they divorced.
    Julie moved away with her mother. In our class photo,
    she stood between Alfonso Ruiz and Ricky Bradley whom
    I couldn't help kiss
    as I kissed her when no one was looking.

"When I get old," I ask my youngest son, "will you still kiss me?"
    Without taking his arms from around my neck,
    he says, "You're old now."

When my sons are in grade school, Grandma takes me to lunch
    to tell me, no matter what my father says,
    "You can come to my house anytime."

She holds my arm on the way to her car and tells
about a kid hitting him in the head with a board.
When we kiss good-bye, she cries and
says, "Be kind to him."

The more seniors who graduate, the better an underclassmen's chances
    of getting a girlfriend. One February night in my junior year,
    Andrea and I sat on the lifeguard stand at Little Solana,
    high winter tides on the bluff below.
    Soft kisses, gentle on her braces that a moment later
    hooked on my sweater.

On the chair in my dorm at College of the Siskiyous,
    a pink ribbon and a note:
        "Bring this back to me if you want. Monica."

It was two summers before I would have a driver's license.
    I spent July at my Aunt's on Mission Bay but
    not with my Aunt. Under the diving barge,
    I held on to a crossbeam and Shira held on to me,
    her legs wrapped around me under the water.
    Her older sister swam out and said
    her father would kill me if
    he could swim.
    Shira spent the rest of the day on the beach,
    crying on a blanket with him.
    He had a mustache like Omar Shariff's.
    I stayed in the water up to my knees until they left.

For Every Too Little, a Too Much

To make my wife less anxious
about my stacks of papers in her office,
your letters, Dad, were the first I recycled,
unread. She begged me not to read another
after what you sent the second time you left me.

Into every holiday, a little highway.
Before that Thanksgiving dinner
I'd been rambunctious about Reagan,
remember? I'd rudely punctuated your lecture
with a request to see your clip file,
your book or someplace where your conservative
blather didn't fill your mouth
like a stone you couldn't spit.

For so much uncut grass, a little less sky.
I let you go a second time,
and you finally wrote letters like water,
telling me not to talk to my half-sister.
I admit I read eight or nine words,
hoping the tone would change, but
I could never climb lower than
the rung of your first legal threat.

Now your grandsons look at Iraq.
Onto every holiday, a hat.
How about a helmet?
Vietnam, I tell them, is the way
to know Grandad. Ah, the peril of family values.
And your patriots talk
to make themselves deaf
so they don't hear
those they devour.

I thought about burning
your letters in the barbeque
but recycled them because
I know how you hate "eco-think."

So from every little madness, a little more.

Goat Laughter

Evacuating down Paradise Mountain,
our trucks and trailers loaded with livestock
jammed to a stop.
In front of me, in the bed of a pickup,
one goat mounted the other.

I looked north not so much in shame, but
to gauge how long before the firestorm rolled over
this little white stucco community scattered in the brush,
now brought bumper to bumper by flames and smoke,

then back to the goats humping as if life depended on it.
Perhaps smoke reminded them of barbeques,
an incense that told them to get to the work of survival.

Though most of us escaped our cage of flames,
that fire underlined civilization's limits.

Now driving home into the cul-du-sac, I swear I hear
laughter in the ashes lifted by the slightest filthy breeze.

Coca-Cola Is Guilt

I sip it slowly, no straw,
just lift the glass flared wide at the top
like Nagasaki
or Hiroshima,
a trademark recognizable worldwide.

Ah, the myths:
    Coke dissolves nails left lying in it.
    Aldolfo Calero and Vincente Fox walked on it.
    It contained cocaine, analgesic for the masses.
I swallow and believe.

It presents itself wherever I go:
    Washes down fast food I eat as
    as I drive between jobs.
    It lifts my mood and carries me through the afternoon;
    safer to drink overseas than water.

If rum is Cuba in the Cuba Libre,
Coke is the freedom of
"Both mother & daughter
working for the Yanqui dollar."

Yes, as I sip the sweet sticky guilt
that explodes on the surface,
that explodes in commercials that
would "like to teach the world to sing"
and to listen to "the pause that refreshes"
exploding in the glass of fizz I lift,
the pizzazz of the otherwise flat "real thing,"
carbonation rising like fireworks in a dark night,
exploding in my face.

Silver Surfaces

A parachutist was the first to notice
as he plunged through the clouds
that he knocked loose silver dust.

They built towers to mine storms and soon
every stylish plate, every fancy car and
dance floor on the veranda was made from

silver linings, yet no matter how we buffed
and shined them, the silver surfaces had
little to reflect except darkening clouds overhead

Last Love

The dust and sweat that was he and she,
filth that was one part him, one part her,
what they brought home from their affairs,
they paid a woman to clean away on Mondays.

One Tuesday afternoon in July,
as he sat on the immaculately made bed,
she ran into the house, out of breath,
stripped off her bra and shorts
and stood before him glazed only in
a sweat he had nothing to do with.

She had run into an honest moment,
a gift of her naked self profaned by
its own death, and she offered it to him
her body now different from when they met.

Despite all the cells of himself he'd lost,
what was alive in him recognized her and
his blood rose like a tide from the other side of the world.
What overwhelmed them,
rolled from her to him and back,
and filled their porous flesh full
was a sense of love's momentum and
the friction of time together.

The Next Dream

The father lies in bed on his left side,
his chest pressed to the back of the mother,
his right arm on her right hip.
He begins his nights on his belly,
so gravity lets his breaths fall from his mouth
without snoring.

But sometime after his first dream,
he awakes and checks the clock.
The loneliness of his dream logic
turns him toward her.

His right arm lies over the hip because
she has said it gets too heavy on her shoulder.
His right leg scissors forward and crosses over her left,
so his knee bends in behind hers.

With her left hand, she takes his right
and some circuit between them closes.
It took years to discover this position
that they sometimes hold for hours.

In the father's next dream,
they never wake,
an earthquake collapses the world over them.
Archaeologists who uncover them argue
in their distant language:
were they frightened together in their last moment
or were they in love?
After tongues dissolve,
can choreography of their bones say
enough about the force of love ?
He dreams we would be blessed
if only our bones survive.

Tuolumne Lines

On the river, reflected clouds
hold back images of boulders below;

likewise, the haze of this page shows only
pencil tip and the poem that follows.

From the shore, where lichen couldn't hold a rock
together, an armful of granite fell underwater,

the shards as hidden as entwined roots of grass in
the meadow where I left two strands of hair,

so I'll always know where they are.
The wind sets ripples on the reflection, so

from this vibrant distortion I lift my eyes
to the tree line broken by gray granite.

In the song of mountain ridges,
amidst the notes of pine and cedar,

rock outcroppings are rests while below
riversong reconciles broken boulders.

My Brother's Nightmare

> *Of old the world on dreaming fed;*
> *gray truth is now her painted toy.*
>   —W.B. Yeats

After Ted Turner laid off my little brother who
color-keyed black & white films,
I consoled him by buying the beers while
silently and with ecstatic guilt I rejoiced for the classic
flashes in the dark that would haunt new generations.

As soon as my brother stopped lamenting, I planned to preach that
Turner's dream of Charles Foster Kane in Christmas red & green
cost a fortune in imagination, more than any tycoon could truly afford.

The psychological fact that most dreams play in black & white with
no source of light haunts my brother:
from steel and glass gray sparkles,
what makes all those shadows.

He, however, tied a rainbow around my eyes,
insisting Bedford Falls was more wonderful with
Mary and George Bailey jitterbugging into a pool of blue
and with Zuzu's petals in pink extreme close-up.
These colors awakened me not to Pottersville's squalor but
to *Pleasantville*'s nightmare of technological firepower and
the smug pigmented engineering of contemporary enlightenment,
present-tense delusion being more dangerous than nostalgia.

"Black is not the only evil color," my brother said with a wink.
In *The Maltese Falcon*, I made Brigid O'Shaughnessy's eyes
the same green as yours for all those pranks you pulled on me."

I didn't speak but poured us more amber glasses to see through:
on the bar TV, a general's khakis had the same tint as my $20 bill.
I closed my evil green eyes while listening to more horrifying tales of
the Frankenstein creature tortured with real orange flame
and taking Dorothy home forever to a Kansas
with fields of emerald in spring but still
no escape for Toto when he finally faces Mrs. Gulch and the Sheriff.
Let's assume the little dog's blood is red.

Difficult Colors

In the hardware store by the wood stoves coolly on display
stand the color kiosks, the paint samples, windows that
      slide open for me to other places and times:
            Whitestone,
                  Moonshine,
                        Gray Horse.
We need no rainbows to crack the world into promise.
I come across Whale Gray and know I've seen only
      one migrating off the broken California coast.
            Does a color survive its namesake?

In the greens, I pull out a dollar to see the color we live for.
It is nothing like Amazon Moss or
      trees transformed into Green Gables.
Most of the green is on the bill's backside,
      Lafayette Green, to be exact, a place I've never visited.

The real color of money is gray, call it "Ethical Silver."

Seashells in the scrollwork become
      fiddlehead ferns, fists raised against winter,
           a jumbled metaphor from the weave of ecology.

On the front, under the etching, the paper appears off-white,
      a young gull's wings beneath storm clouds.
On the face, only the Treasury seal and serial numbers are green,
      to be precise, Jade Green, giving the currency a stony indifference.

The futility of naming any color promises poets work because
      things change with weather and the position of light.

So the gull's feathers darken after her second year,
        the same gull who looks less silver inland under December storms
              than she does above the glare rising off July waves.

Coats of paint disappear into thirsty plaster, the way people and places do
        when anyone stops telling stories about them.

So to all the names of the endangered and extinct,
        may you be more than colors, more than imagination
            may the grays and greens of dollars never mean more than
                what they could never create, what they
                    can never replace on this rare planet,
                      more than poems can name.

Hymn of Enough

All the animals we change for money,
all the sacrifices we've made for change,
all the dollars that float on the current of blood—
                    bullets for teeth,
                            jets for wings
                                    bombs for claws—
make me stand like Jeremiah in the temple gate and
shout there must be one place where we deny our flesh,
where it is on earth as it is in heaven,
where the lion lives by the words of enough,
by the thought of being more than lion,
one place where lion sustains lions of perpetual compassion,
one place without hunger except to be lions in the sun,
lions on the savannah, lions to laze and roar
when the sky of silence calls for roaring.

So to all the fans cheering the troops,
"Bravo, bravo, bravo, Charlie" is not applause,
as if every stop-loss order were an encore and
the troops were sheep in Chaplin's *Modern Times*
or cattle in Hawk's *Red River*,
or extras in the cheerleader-in-chief's *Bring It On*.
It's time to bring them home,
shut down one ring in this circus and
let the clown rest his smile.

So for all the veterans of Charlie Company
still looking for Charlie in Vietnam,
for all the cold warriors looking for their peace dividend, instead
see Rumsfeld's right hand reach for Saddam's once, twice, sold!
See Norriega's post-School-of-the-Americas doctoral thesis in Panama.
See Osama's Freedom Fighters return to the CIA offices in the WTC.
In this jihad of musical-evil-empire-chairs,

may you learn to love your enemy as yourself;
make your move on your lover for old times' sake;
may you find what you seek,
and when you get some, get some, get some,
may it be enough at last, at last, at last.

And to the endangered lasts:
the last polar bear, the last spotted owl,
the last Channel Island fox, the last Thornmint,
the last Alameda whipsnake and leatherback sea turtle,
                                  and island night lizard,
to the last Vine Hill manzanita under a concrete foundation
                                  in Vine Hill Estates,
to the last Long Valley milk-vetch under the pavement
                                  of Long Valley Parkway,
to the ghost of the last marsh sandwort below the surface
                                  of Marina del Mar,
to the last San Clemente Sparrow, the last Belding's sparrow,
the ghost of the Santa Barbara song sparrow
we beg forgiveness for being more than lions,
for not lying down with you,
for getting some and then some more
for singing in your silence
*Why should I feel discouraged,**
why should the shadows fall
when we know,
we know damn well why we
long for heaven and home
when we make creation our dominion.
With fewer sparrows for God to put Her eye on
it becomes a smoke blue gospel that makes me
sing because I'm happy,
I sing because I'm free.

His eye looks for *the sparrow*
but all he finds is *me*
singing on a pile of bones,
the skeleton inside my flesh resonating in familiarity with
the fact sacrifice is survival's flip side,
the ghosts who haunt this meat,
the shiver in the stillness,
the nothing amidst enough.

* Sung to "His Eye Is on the Sparrow" by Civilla Martin and Charles Gabriel.

Invasive Hunger

Home from summer vacation, I opened the freezer
where thousands of dead Argentinean Ants
peppered the frozen fish and ice cubes.

Drought and a decade of warm winters
made them desperate. Now it's my turn.

I try to poison the queen,
but she sends her progeny into the kitchen
for grains of sugar, drops of honey, unwashed dishes.

I resist her colonizing my home but
can't carry the poison down the supply line to her throne.
Odds are I've eaten several of the lives she's sent.
It's horrible.
It's a war, all entrance strategy until
God herself liberates the rains overhead.

Who was the first ant to make the expedition
into the freezer and return to recruit
thousands to hike to their deaths?

Now long after he's gone,
younger sons and nephews
follow the scent as if it were a flag,
not enough reason,
not enough poison
to stop this war. Not enough food
or borders to incite the peace.

Man on the overpass,

his long black hair
unbound down his back,

stands alone above
I-10 between Tucson

and Las Cruces.
The dirt clods dropped

from his fingertips,
unbind on blacktop

to rise in a brown pile
which our speeding van

lifts into a small storm
as we rush east

beneath him on
Christmas Day, 1994.

Creases

Sitting knee-to-knee, I tried to see your face
as a camera lens does, without blinking or touching.
The minutes passed and I didn't plan to remember
the details there but to see them in that *then*:

gray eyes, rise of cheeks, forehead beneath your bangs,
but the edges moved. The lines left from expressions
became creases on a photograph carried in a pocket,
honest details that would become you later.
Did you see the same things in me,
the pulses, the real brutality,
the rippling of lips, nostrils,
waves beneath the muscle and over bone?

A year ago, I saw you with your family as you crossed
5th Street while I waited three cars back at the signal,
too far for me to tell time by the lines on your face,
too far to read any shadow of hesitation reflected at seeing me or
my face with its perfect creases of vice and virtue, where
I'd washed away the dust from suntans and newspaper smudges.
I remembered you with moving edges from that other moment,
and wondered if lines came from my frame of mind
or creasing you as I carried you over years.

Young man pedaling

up the sidewalk
in low gear
during a cloudy year.

Shirt off to show
miracles he built
beneath the scars—
    one slice
    as if someone tried
    to steal his shoulder,
        another cut
        across his belly
        not by a surgeon
        but some illiterate Zorro
    or perhaps the "Z"
    was legible until
the young man
began to build the muscles
under the wound.

Bon Voyage

Mornings, before waking up,
I look around my dream
with its interesting problem,
a cartoon where solutions
hang in the balloons above
our heads, good words,
things that should be said,

but before I can grab a pencil,
morning rams the dock of my bed.
I shatter a bottle of champagne
across its bow and blink my eyes.
Good ideas fizz in my mind.
As I blink again, the dream blurs,
good lines cast off and
the solution pops word by word.

Shell of Heaven

after Rilke

I am not a falcon.
I am not a storm.
I am the song sung by seven generations
that has risen one breath on top
of another.
The singers know I do not reach for God,
that the helix of tones is shaped as they
flow and resonate through the canal of Her ear.

Flow Between Storms

A note from a guitar is a raindrop
that falls from the guitarist's mind,
falls from the electrical storms of
two gray clouds colliding behind the eyes,
through branches of fingertips, fretboard and
strings to splash on someone's eardrum.

A note is a seed with memory
of a limb's sustained reach for sunlight
and a root's grind through dirt to
grasp its fractal: another root.
The rain flows beneath the earth then up through sky.
Songs are trees shaped by the nearest wind and shade.
Listen to the diversity of songs,
the dense tone from a forest-born guitar compared
to open ring of the lone maple in the field.

Guitars are seeds exploding up and across the shell of sky.
The wood grain swirls in remembrance of earth's elements,
resonates with the woodcutter's saw, the crash of its own fall
and the luthier's touch, these fingerprints
fragments of evidence from making music,
a few drops from the storms.

Another Way To Say "God's Eyes"

Another name for family is gravity.
Topography of time and
hydrology of blood brings us here.
From our blindside Mountain lions prey on us.

Gravity brings us through the front door
when this planet spins away from the light.
Some wait for earth to spin toward night,
so they can find the handle and turn.

If home is a womb,
no wonder I never stay long.
Ah, the duty of young honor or
the elderly strength to walk
toward the mountain lion's jaws.

Another name for time is hope.
The writing on the wall is as good as
the last word gets, so let our ceilings be
high with enough wall between door and
window to graffiti the facts.

Change is another name for weather,
which touches us all.
Sunshine is polite if we
switch the subject with each cloud.
Meditating on a storm long
enough to survive will do;
although you can talk about
and finally through it, too.

Hojas y Ojos: Leaves and Eyes

Quepos, Costa Rica

On afternoons, the vacationing couple
sat on the patio, faces turned up
to glimpse a monkey in the rain forest.

They so wanted to see something
with eyes they recognized,
something like themselves amid

the wet oval leaves turned down,
catching light off patio tiles,
beneath them after rain, life reflected.

Witness Trees, 2007

On a Transit Center bench in deep eucalyptus shade,
I remember how long these trees have given so much.

In '65, when I asked about the houses here between them,
my mom said, "That's the Bracero camp," and drove past.

Eucalyptus with nothing to pick, just scent after March rain,
and in August, a harvest of shadows for riders the buses unload.

Men in Trees

Around my home the men in the trees
appeared with certain seasons.
The ladders they climbed had no roots.
Cold mornings, someone broke a crate and
made a fire on the grove road.
The men in the trees picked the fruit,
left circles of ash and sang while they did so.

Did they really sing as they picked the groves?
Sí mon, someone sang in Spanish
even in the afternoon heat.

Before dawn their old bus with ladders on top
rattled up our road.
Soon, the forklift ground the washboards to powder as
it wheeled to slam one wooden bin on another.

But during the quiet heat
when the insects shut up,
someone sang a corrido,
but I imagine, "Muy lejos de ti" (very far from you).

At school, we lifted small cartons of orange juice
to our lips, and I could feel
the men in the trees carrying the sun to us,
the light from the fruit illuminating
faces beneath the broad hat brims.

They were not the trees, but they have become a crop.
Who can harvest and carry it now?
Who can neglect it and let generations of fruit fall to the ground?

Money orders and airmail are no longer enough
on this planet that can't bear one more footprint.
We keep men in trees until branches become firewood
leaving ladders nothing to lean on.
Did anyone believe if they climbed year after year
they would one day reach through the sky
and their families would follow?
Between the rows of stumps,
the living haunt us.
No messiah leads them past the top rung.
No one can carry this harvest of consequences;
no one claims it.
It doesn't rot no matter how hot the sun.

Hotel Carrera, 1974

after a George Stranahan photo

Santiago during Pinochet,
four old people in the lounge
stare out the rectangular window.

No one talks, no glances one to another.
Maybe they already know the faces or
don't care whom they sit with or
this lounge has the only window left:
a frame for a picture of the street.

Or maybe it's a time to be quiet
and watch Chile as if it were a movie,
as if the images in the street weren't real.

After Dusk

Oh-no, my mistaken identity.
Police believe they've profiled me
but don't know my vampiric mind.

I rationalized my belief in flesh,
blood and love. Just because
I wear sunglasses and keep to the shade,

left my home one August night
to split open hearts with mine, doesn't mean
the other creature will break free of my skin.

I never needed a mirror as a mask;
nevertheless, last night I gazed into the police
as they shoved me around the checkpoint.

The jangley cop securely said,
"We know your thirsty kind."
His constipated sidekick punctuated

with an accident-flare to my sternum.
They so longed for my purple of bruises,
but I fanned my lips and yawned;

they flinched politely when
I said, "Sorry, no spare crimes on me.
I just need a nap and some Novocain."

With me packing the blood so deep,
they told me to carry on,
but we all knew it was an escape

after dusk. From their dungeons
of reason they let me go
because they could,

and I glided away, above the dusty sidewalk,
both my shoulders brushing the invisible
corridors inside our national castle.

Crime Medicine

No crime medicine sat on the shelf
above the sink in the house where he grew up.

The weave of fingerprints cushioned his grasp
on the world beside him. As far as

the boundaries of siblings do not dissipate
during life and often not after death,

the constant identity of skin posits
nothing more than evidence of another soul.

So it is the fragments we offer constant strangers
that we would have them identify at cocktail parties

or wherever enemies and accomplices meet.
Nothing was criminal in that kitchen except him.

Dream Damage

When did I allow my son's room to swallow him,
I wonder, passing Rafe's open door. He sits,
black X-Box controller in hand, while on screen
space creatures groan and flop in pools of purple blood.
It takes a moment to realize I watch them die
from Rafe's killer point of view.

He asks this pacifist father to sit and
splits the screen so I have my own gun site
to learn how to plasma-pistol space grunts
protecting Halo's hallways, except
I can't control the toggle. My monitor shows floor,
or so I believe until Rafe clues me, "It's ceiling," just as
my screen blinks blank and cuts to a blue space
creature laughing over my lifeless body.

Rafe laughs in real life as I'm resurrected onscreen
and friendly-fire him into virtual limbo.
"Don't worry about it," he says. "It's only a game,"
as, resurrected, he frags me into electronic after-life.

We play all afternoon and after dinner.
I toggle after him into virtual space. We play so long
our eyes turn rectangular to match our screens.

That night, I dream monsters in corridors that split and merge,
fire pre-emptive bursts into the maze's shadows,
afraid I'll recognize any collateral damage.
In *my* nightmare I need to find Rafe in the game,
know we kept the corridors of our minds open
no matter the conscious costs of making a home.

The Reagan Memorial Poem

Mr. President, given your medical & political history
the "Reagan Memorial" anything seemed in poor taste to me.
But after seeing your spirit drifting proudly along your freeways,
through so many schools and over your own aircraft carrier,
the planes taking off and disappearing like many facts,
I now bow to peer pressure and offer this memorial poem.

I saw your funeral in the National Cathedral,
      the camera at a bird's-eye angle
the same as God must've had:
      ring of mourners around your casket,
mise-en-scène as if by Busby Berkeley,
      the way you would've wanted it.
Your coffin sat to the bottom of the encircling crowd, so
your funeral looked like the smiley face gone seriously blind.

How appropriate, I thought, not the blindness,
but the respectful space around your coffin,
for it was there the ghosts began to drift:
      the Iranians whom Iraq gassed with military aid you
      initiated over Amnesty International's cries. Listen,
      we can still hear them weeping for Kurds, Kuwaitis and,
      of course, our own.
      How good of you to sit up in the casket and salute them.

      Then came the Nicaraguenses, some carrying
      their diaphanous limbs lopped off by the Contras.
      In grace, they piled eyes, ears, breasts,
      genitalia and tongues into your coffin.

      The Salvadoreños wearing neutralized expressions
      followed the Afghanis whom your freedom fighters liberated
      from life and any happy pursuit not
      allowed by a literal reading of the Koran.

>   Finally, the Guatamaltecos crowded
>   comfortably around your coffin;
>   they'd been practicing in mass graves at least
>   since you restored military aid in '81.

Did you recognize the ghost of Bishop Juan Gerardi?
>   You were deep in the delusions of Alzheimer's in '98 when
>   a graduate of Fort Benning's School of the Americas
>   bludgeoned Bishop Gerardi for counting Guatemala's dead.
>   Genocide plus one.

How big of you not to make a fuss when
Gerardi helped you from your coffin and absolved you,
you not remembering what you did
or repenting and all that.

Filling your coffin with their broken bodies, they
floated beside you as you rode behind the caisson,
the nation honoring you in death as you had lived:
remembering nothing but good things:
>   how you held the picket line at the Warsaw shipyards,
>   how you stared down the Kremlin guards who took you
>   hostage, how you freed Tibet and
>   personally piloted the Dali Lama home on Air Force One.

It must have been at that moment of the procession,
you riding backwards yet comfortable in your old boots,
all of us suffering Sympathy Alzheimer's,
that your mind was healed and
you understood you were on your way to heaven,
to spend eternity with the ghosts flowing beside you,
and that was when you began to cue the horse back
along the trail, so the bullets would revert to dollars,

the ink on the executive order flowing into the pen in your hand.
God bless that horse,
even with you sitting backwards in the saddle like that,
it wanted to obey your cues and turn from the grave,
but, alas, the soldier leading it had other orders.

Radiate

In the Memory Market

People in the mall carried their terror well,
most stopped in to purchase, not exchange.
Business was good.
Everyone had the new bin-Laden-at-Large.7;
I, however, wanted the kinder, gentler
      "Freedom-Fighter.1" version.

Or I'd trade my 2003 Anthrax Scare for an '83 Saddam,
you know, the old handshake model.
"Sorry," said the smiley old clerk
      behind the Memory Mart counter.
"We're all out. Perhaps you'd like to
      take the new Hugo Chavez for a spin?"
"No thanks," I said. "Never had any luck buying Latin America."
On the counter I unloaded
      a million Operation Gatekeeper detainees.
"You advertised these as 'new and improved,
but they're no different than
      the Operation Wetback version of '54," I said,
dumping out a million more. "Which is which?"

Although the clerk's dark hair had held up better than his skin,
his grandfatherly smile never faltered.
"What you want is the bigger-better-fence shareware," he said.
I shook my head. "Didn't work for ancient China or Rome."

"Then you must be a collector," the clerk said,
      leading back to the storeroom.
"Ah, how about this Arbenz overthrow from '54?
Those were the days," he said,
      glowing while holding out a spool of piano wire.
Didn't this clerk use his own product?
"I said nothing from Latin America.

I'm already carrying five, no, make that six decades of Castro
and they just keep getting heavier despite all your upgrades."

I saw pity in the old clerk's eyes.
"What you need is a win," he said.
From between The Treaty of Versailles and
a chunk of the Berlin Wall on the top shelf,
he lifted down a shah-shaped piece of paper.
"The Mosedegh coup of '53, very rare," he said,
placing an oil rights contract in my hands.
"Look at the signature," the clerk said.

I squinted at the blank over Mosedegh's name.
"It's empty," I said.
"Exactly," the clerk said.
"The best history ignores the consequences."

"Too heavy," I said, trying to hand it back.
"Just give me a dozen Iraqi IEDs."
 "Sorry," the clerk said. "One doesn't work without the other."
"Well, I can't afford them both," I said holding out the coup.
"I know," said the clerk, his smile holding like a beehive hair-do.
"Nevertheless, it's yours. You own this store.
        I just keep it for you."

I heard my merchandise wheeze as he repacked it.
I didn't feel any lighter, but the blowback
        balanced my posture
so my war on terror no longer slouched
        so much toward Santiago '73.
"What you need now is some amnesia to go with that order,"
the clerk said ushering me toward the door.
"And that you can buy almost anywhere in the mall."

Darlin', when our figure-eight starts

and when it ends is difficult to say. For me,
swells begin in different cells,

tides come in from without,
merge with currents my ear remembers,
an undertow pulls me from spine to skull.

Not a close-up spliced into a blue movie.
Darlin', we could map our darknesses.
Shadow frames our places beyond the flame.

The navigation, I've forgotten.
The momentum of tides turns
me toward you, always coming.

Our currents reverse at the crest, and
I lose sight of you in the sun, where
waves push into the sky, and sky presses back.

We pass through light-blinded and
circle to where we know we'll touch,
Darlin'...

The Answer

Whose SoCal curls beside my SoCal?
Whose Escondido hides with mine?
Who walks fearlessly near Poison Oak,
      weaves her steps between its branches in any season?
Where is the trailhead that leads through her thoughts?
What is the landscape I know,
      that I walk with attention to topography?

How necessary are her steps through our home?
Who could map the streets of my mind?
Whose memory is the city we build
      where I want to become lost?
What laughter in the next room is home?
What voice is a song moving me from my mundane worries
      to the divine in this world?
Who could draw our sons together on such fine days?

Whose footprints overlap mine on the trails?
Whose feet rub together in her sleep?
Whose green enchiladas burn my kisses?
Who is the taste of damp earth in gold tequila, so
      her kiss inebriates me?

Whose face is a galaxy open to and
      beyond me,
      the more years I navigate by it,
      the more mysterious it becomes—
      even in moments of completion?
What skin beside my own maps my life?
Whose eyes have become planets in my sky,
      their orbit through my days marking the hours?

Light in All Directions

I felt your gaze all day as you drove the road toward me.
That night in the observatory, we leaned into the telescope and
held our breath to focus on Jupiter with five moons,
lit like half-closed blind eyes,
all that old light taking eight minutes to reach us on
one of the planets close enough to catch the light from a star.

Then you found Saturn and made out the rings standing on knife-point
and the band of shadow,
the dark older than the light,
the same dark just beyond the porch lamp,
the same constant dark between any two people.

A star sends its light in all directions
like a king dispatching a navy that sinks in the crossing except
one ship that arrives as you have
to make new whatever light survives.
Under that dome, dark so people can see stars,
I leaned against the wall and only you and your light fell onto me.

Author Bio

Brandon Cesmat teaches literature & writing at several colleges in Southern California. His first book, *Driven into the Shade,* received a San Diego Book Award. His short story collection *When Pigs Fall in Love & Other Stories* is from Caernarvon Press.

He is an active teaching artist in California Poets in the Schools (CPITS) and an active member in Teaching Artists Organize (TAO).

Cesmat harvests brush every summer with his wife and their three sons at their home just above Paradise Creek in Valley Center, California.

www.ingramcontent.com/pod-product-compliance
Lightning Source LLC
Chambersburg PA
CBHW070304100426
42743CB00011B/2345